You Have The Power To Excel Irrespective Of Your Background

Insights into your breakthrough despite the odds

Simeon O. Edosomwan, Ph.D.

Copyright © 2019 Simeon O. Edosomwan, Ph.D. All rights reserved. No part of this book can be reproduced in any form without the written permission of the author and its publisher.

Contents

Dedication 9

QUICK INSIGHTS ABOUT EXCELLING 11

Chapter 1 17

You Can Excel 17

Chapter 2 25

Educational Matters...25

Chapter 3 49

Challenges 49

Chapter 4 71

Fighting For Your Life 71

Chapter 5 87

Despite The Failures: Try Again........................87

Chapter 6 107

Perception & Productivity..............................107

Chapter 7 123

How Success Works 123

Chapter 8 141

Voice of Hope..141

Chapter 9: Special Reflection 161

Dedication

I dedicate this book to my late father Samson E. Edosomwan. He impacted me with, his wisdom and taught me the true meaning of overcoming life's adversities.

I know he is watching over me behind the veil. God bless you BABA.

QUICK INSIGHTS ABOUT

EXCELLING

1. Understand that you cannot choose what life will place in your path, but you can control who you are and what you want to become.

    "Some are born great, some achieve greatness, and others have greatness thrust upon them." ~ William Shakespeare

2. To excel, you must build your identity capital because humans are capable and can do the most remarkable things. But great accomplishments incubate over an extended period.

    "do something that adds value to who you are, do

> something that is an investment on whom you might want to be next."
> ~Meg Jay

3. **People who excel pay specific attention to their experiences and the experience of others; the key is to learn from them.**
   > *"experience is the richest resource for adults' learning."* ~ Eduard Christian Lindeman

4. **Our perceptions determine our productivity.**
   > *"A pessimist sees the difficulty in every opportunity, an optimist sees the opportunity in every difficulty."* ~ Winston Churchill

5. **Failing is part of the experience of people who excel. The difference, they keep trying**

until they succeed beyond expectation.

> "I've missed more than 9000 shots in my career. I've lost almost 300 games. 26 times, I've been trusted to take the game winning shot and missed. I've failed over and over and over again in my life. And that is why I succeed." ~ Michael Jordan

6. **Unfortunately, challenges and adversity are part of the human life. We have to learn the skills to overcome adversity.**

> "It's not what happens to you in life that matters. It's how you respond to what happens to you that makes a difference". ~ Zig Ziglar

7. **People who excel believed that they have a shot at the American dream if they work tirelessly with purpose, hope, and**

determination. The American dream is a promise that, regardless of your circumstances of birth or position, you have a shot at success. This principle is applicable not just in America, but wherever you find yourself.

> *"The American Dream is that dream of a land in which life should be better and richer and fuller for everyone, with opportunity for each according to ability or achievement. It is not... a dream of motor cars and high wages merely, but a dream of social order in which each man and each woman shall be able to attain to the fullest stature of which they are innately capable, and be recognized by*

others for what they are, regardless of the fortuitous circumstances of birth or position." ~ James Truslow Adams

Chapter 1

You Can Excel

Have you ever felt helpless and dejected? Have you ever been told that you could not achieve anything worthwhile because you are not the brightest or from a powerful background? Do you sometimes doubt yourself? Maybe it is because of your life circumstances, situations, and experiences that you tend to question your potential? I encourage you to do this no more because you have THE POWER TO EXCEL IRRESPECTIVE OF YOUR BACKGROUND. If you're like me, maybe you often second guess yourself. You have some people in your life who tell you that it's not possible. Knowing where you're coming from, some things seem so far out of reach. But I tell you today, you have the power to excel. This power residing within you is unlimited and unstoppable. Trust me, you certainly can't choose all that life will put in your path, but I believe you can control who you are and what you want to become. I know this because humans are capable and can do the most remarkable and incredible things. To excel doesn't mean you have to be perfect, excelling is a daily process of doing things well and overtime you become better and continue to better your best. One of the extraordinary things I have discovered about life is that to excel irrespective of what life puts on your path, you must seek to do a little more when you have less, and develop a special kind of identity that will help you excel irrespective of your odds. This identity that will help you excel is not of crisis but of capital. And imagine for a second, who can touch that man or woman who has capital? I don't think there is anyone!

American Clinical psychologist, Meg Jay, who specializes in adult development, in her TED talk described this unique identity I am asking you to develop in terms of having some *"identity capital."* By identity capital, she explained, "do something that adds value to who you are, do something that is an investment in whom you might want to be next." If you pursue this path, I promise you, the difference personally and professionally in your life, in no distant time will speak volumes in return. I've experienced it, I have lived this philosophy, and continue to make this idea I am asking you to try my own central tenet. It is amazing how it has literally changed my life, and this can also be your testimony.

Throughout history, the story of the world is filled with men and women who have turned nothing into something, going from less to having more, something ordinary to something extraordinary, and turning impossibilities into possibilities. They are all documented in the books, you can read about them, and you probably know of someone I am talking about that turned nothing into something. American 16th president, Abraham Lincoln is one of such extraordinary individuals. He is known as the great emancipator who preserved the union we all have today as the United States. He had a rough childhood, lost is mother at the age of nine and as a lawyer, he lost several cases, yet he did not let his failures or humble beginnings define him. He is known as one of America's heroic Leaders for his bravery and ability to not give up despite the odds. I am not saying we can all become Abraham Lincoln, but there is something unique about his life tales you and I can learn from. I believe each of us, in our own unique ways, are powerful and do indeed possess the potential to turn nothing into something. Although you must allow yourself to experience this extraordinary process that will enable you to turn baby steps into great strides. Just like me at first, a lot of people might feel inadequate and make excuses for not stepping into their greatness. They are afraid to storm the world lest they fail. Well, this attitude cannot possibly pay off in the long run. Because your playing small, does not serve the world, nor does it serve your needs or purposes. Besides, what excuse is good enough for not maximizing your potential or making your life more fulfilling? American author and New York mega-bestseller Marianne Williamson correctly stated, *"Our deepest fear is not that we are inadequate. Our deepest fear is that we are powerful beyond measure. It is our light, not our darkness that most frightens us."* I could not agree with her more. I believe that you and I are powerful beyond any quantification. The intent of this book is not to mislead you to believe that life is easy, but to show you through my own vulnerabilities and life experiences that, despite the ups and downs we all experience, you are magnificent and you indeed have the power to excel irrespective of your background. All that you might need is to learn and apply some basic life philosophies that will ensure you stay strong during the good times and most important during moments of adversity. These philosophies you might need to learn will be useful to help you pursue your purpose with diligence, and empower you with the capacity to not cave in when life moments look scary. Are you ready to read my story? I hope your answer is a resounding yes, yes. Here is something special for you to think about and work on as you begin this life-changing journey:

A) What have you ever done that was scary at first? How did you do it?
B) What can you do a little bit more today to advance your purpose?
C) What are you doing now to add value to yourself each day?
D) What are your fears, and how can you conquer them?

Chapter 2

Educational Matters

In my own imperfect yet determined life I have come to realize that if you look beyond your immediate circumstances and seek opportunities, they will come no matter how long it may take. Typically, great accomplishments incubate over an extended period and take time. I know this because there were things I have always wanted to achieve in my life, but they did not happen in a sprint, they took an elongated period of time to accomplish. At first, it seemed the journey would be too long and unattainable, but with vision, intentionality, and tenacity, I now find myself achieving them, despite my background. When I was in my early teens, one of the major goals I decided on and I set for myself was that education was going to be the path I would pursue. This seemed especially important in those days in Nigeria when all we heard over and over in popular slogans was that *"education is the key to success."* Although I must admit, we weren't shown how this education would bring the much-articulated success. Since I wasn't from a privileged background, education for me looked like a means to fulfillment. I wasn't going to let this slice of pie of educational success pass me by. It was my decision and realization to seek knowledge through formal education that helped me grow up confidently believing that things would be great for me and my family someday. I graduated from the great University of Benin in Nigeria and decided that I was going to attend graduate school in the United States. It was actually in 2005 during my undergraduate studies in college when I first dreamed of the idea of obtaining a doctoral degree. This idea seemed crazy given that up to that point, nobody in my family had completed a college education let along anticipate a doctoral degree.

At times, life can be very funny, so be very careful what you ask for because your mere wish and aspiration can quickly snowball into something real and life-changing. It all starts with a little idea. Indeed all great accomplishments start with a simple idea.

Academic experts and scholars have have shown that over half of doctoral students in America and elsewhere around the world who begin their doctoral journey never actually make it to completion. You probably know of someone in this category, and if you don't, you will probably meet someone someday who began a Ph.D. study but never completed it. My decision to obtain a Ph.D. degree was not because I believed I possessed some special kind of intelligence to undertake this path of rigorous learning. I believed that I was strong enough to persist, and that I had enough hope to withstand the many setbacks that are common for doctoral students.

When I first started my doctoral education journey, I had many acquaintances say to me that they could never imagine studying for a Ph.D., asking me "what do you even want with a Ph.D.?" Some of my close friends even ridiculed my decision and wondered if I was in my right senses. I remember one day I shared with one of my friends how hard my Ph.D. studies were becoming for me, and he sarcastically laughed at me and remarked, wasn't I the one who decided to undergo this study, good luck, and stop complaining.

On my own part, when things weren't going the way I had envisioned, I would get frustrated, and too many times I also questioned and criticized myself until I had nothing left to whine about.

My vulnerability notwithstanding, let me also praise myself in that as scary as my Ph.D. journey was, I continued to show up. I still went to the classes, even when I did not feel like going. When my P.h.D colleagues had gone home from class, I stayed back and read a little bit more, even when I felt like going home myself and not opening the books.

The truth is that, for me, education has always been a dream and a desire. It has been my passport for adding value to myself and the lens through which I was going to see the world. Zig Ziglar, the world-renowned motivational speaker once stated, nothing thrills him more than to see a person who decides to go back to school to earn a degree or learn a new skill. Absolutely, I agree with him. I sincerely believe that people who take the extra pain to go to school, learn a new skill, go to seminars, and continue to develop intellectually have a better shot at excelling in life, irrespective of their background. Conversely, those people who ignore the opportunity to learn or engage in a knowledge-based activity, who never open their books, never go to classes, and never attend lectures may begin to find learning difficult if not impossible. What an unfortunate loss of potential!

Now, there are people who might question the relevance of education today. They may question the need to attend school, given the many challenges that confront formal educational systems, including its affordability and quality. They may question educational relevance and cite that there are many life-building skills that are not taught in the classroom. Some might even go as far as to say things like, I know of someone such as Bill Gates who hasn't completed school, yet he has become very successful financially. And while Bill Gates' financial success is unquestionable, I bet you, Bill Gates case is a rare exception to the norm.

Interestingly, you would be shocked to learn how much people such as Bill Gates invest in their learning. Do you know of the millions of dollars Bill Gate invests every year to promote education? Why would he himself, the self-made man, make these investments if formal education has no relevance, or is not valuable? Don't get me wrong, the pushback and tough questions about education are quite understandable, and such social critique is necessary to demand a better educational system for everyone.

The question is not even whether education is relevant or not, because it obviously is! The question is whether contemporary education is fulfilling its purpose? Today there seems to be so much focus on obtaining a degree and a certification mentality, rather than focussing on what students are actually learning from school to help them handle life challenges. Edward Malloy once stated, *"A college degree is not a sign that one is a finished product but an indication a person is prepared for life."* I think this is the proper perspective with which to approach formal education. Education gets your foot in the door to success and expands your mind to what is possible. Indeed, education is meant to expand your mind and help you prepare for the life ahead. It is not intended to make you a finished product, because you can never learn all that you need to know about life in four or five years. By many measures, I just think the validity of education in our lives simply cannot be disputed, and it is worth your involvement and investment. Nelson Mandela stated, *"a good head and good heart are always a formidable combination. But when you add to that a literate tongue or pen, then you have something very special."* How special it can really be for someone to get an education that will empower them to become the best version of themselves.

For me, my education has been far more than the degrees I have received from school. It has been through my involvement in higher learning that my mind has expanded, and I developed a vision of how knowledge can change my life. I began to think about life in ways I probably never would have even dared to imagine before. If you really want to excel, I suggest you get deeply involved in the process of education and truly seek to be transformed by your learning experiences.

Believe me when I say to you that over 90 percent of inmates in the American prison system have limited formal education. That alone tells me that without education it becomes far too easy to be attracted to crime, nefarious activities, and wayward living. When I worked briefly in a state correctional facility in North Dakota, I witnessed the devastating outcomes of poor choices due to the lack of education. A prisoner once said to me, committing crimes and going from prison to prison was all he he had ever known. He had never gone to school beyond the first grade. This prisoner related this information to me during a training session I was conducting with new inmates. As I think of my encounter with this grown man that day, I can now fully understand why the famous French writer, Victor Hugo stated, *"he who opens a school door closes a prison."* Apart from the overwhelming correlation between a lack of education and crime, the research is pretty clear that there is also a positive relationship between education and upward social mobility. Nelson Mandela described this best by stating,

> *"Education is the great engine of personal development. It is through education that the daughter of a peasant can become a doctor, that the son of a mineworker can become the head of the mine that a child of a farm worker can become the president of a great nation. It is what we make out of what we have, not what we are given, that*

> *separates one person from another."*

You are right to think I am one of the beneficiaries of education who this quote may apply to. For me, my education wasn't an option, rather it was a matter of time and necessity to help me prepare for the future ahead of me. Luckily for me, I was fortunate to love school from a very young age, but I must confess I wasn't the brightest of students. I recall when I was young, my father would make sure that every night my siblings and I read something before we went to bed. Most times, I would just pretend to be reading, use the book as a shield to cover my face, and then just go to sleep. Despite this youthful mediocrity and defiance, my father continued to push and encourage the ritual of reading. He was also big on and loved learning as well. When I was in primary school, what is commonly referred to as elementary school here in America, my father would drive my siblings and me in his old tortoise car (1967 Classic Volkswagen Beetle) to the bookstore at forestry road in Benin City to purchase our textbooks prior to the commencing of each school year. This was a big luxury at the time, because not every child in my community got this kind of royal treatment. I knew this because even after school had already resumed, some of the kids in my class had not received their books, and the teacher would threaten to send them back home to their parents the next day if their books weren't bought. Some of my classmates even begged to sit with me so they could read from my books. In those early years, I simply cannot remember a time when my father did not go out of his way to ensure our books were ready before the school session started. In his room closet, my father kept stacks of writing notebooks he bought from the now-closed and bankrupt famous Ethiope publishers in Benin City. Whenever any of us needed any writing material or a book, his closet was just around the corner. But we dared not go into his closet to take a precious new notebook by ourself! We had to ask him first and justify why we needed one. Otherwise, we would "be in the soup" and experience my father's discipline!

Oh, how I loved those days when my father drove us with his tortoise car to the bookstore. While on the ride, our youthful exuberance was in full display. We were being children, being silly, and just being happy. I, in particular, remember cheering and jumping in the back of my father's tortoise car as he drove. He would instruct me to sit down and stop being loud! After a little while, I would stand again anyways and repeat the very same behavior I had been asked to stop, because I was just a child, and knew no better as a kid.

Added to this foundation of getting my books ready for school, I grew up watching my father read every night. He never missed a night except if something was wrong. I must be the first to admit that his ritual of reading paid off for him as well. Even without any postsecondary education experience, my father's knowledge was simply astonishing and amazing. I remember one experience shortly before my father died, he invited me over to come read a passage from the book of proverbs to him because of his bad sight. As I read this particular passage of the scripture to him I missed a word. When I concluded reading, praising myself thinking I had done a great job, he protested and brought my attention back stating I had not read the passage correctly. He demanded I go back and re-read the whole entire passage of this scripture to him again. In all honesty, I believe if I possess a quarter of the knowledge my father had, I will be able to move mountains.

Every night, when I woke up to use the bathroom, my father was right there at his usual reading table studying as if he had exams to write the next day. To this day, I still wonder how my father disciplined himself to such a regimental reading schedule and stuck to it. The benefit for me was that seeing my father's reading culture instilled in me the desire to want to learn.

Come to think of it, my desire did not emerge out of the blue. Modern psychological research has clearly demonstrated that what we see, listen to, and read do largely influence, as well as drive our actions. I am correct to say that what I saw my father do in terms of reading every night deeply influenced my actions. The grateful part of myself dedicates most of my accomplishments to my father for his intelligence and all that he taught me. I could never comprehend all at once, but I also saw that he had never really even had a chance to go to school. Instead, he worked hard, and he passed his dream on to me, and thus I wanted to go to school. I wanted to get a Ph.D. Indeed, I wanted to excel.

When I eventually grew older and made it to college, my passion for education was further telling. While in college, I met some incredible professors whom I admired because of the way they carried themselves, and their knowledge disposition was priceless. That was all I needed for further confirmation of my life's direction. That did it all for me. So much so, I wanted to be like my professors in college. As a result, I decided to pursue learning as far as I could. Perhaps my life would also become like the lives of those I so greatly admired. This decision became a reality fourteen years later, from the time I had first conceived this crazy idea of obtaining a Ph.D., to my dream becoming a lived reality. I now have the Ph.D. that I set my focus on achieving long ago. When I look at my life's journey and how it all started for me, it seems it should have been impossible to have thought or believed that I could accomplish what I have now, because nothing in my life history forecasted that I would become a doctoral degree recipient. But it happened for me, and it can also happen for you.

So, if you live well with focused intention, a specific goal in mind, and put in a lot of effort to see to the actualization of what you're doing, I guarantee you, regardless of your background, you are going to excel beyond what you ever imagined. My Ph.D. experience taught me this life-changing lesson, and I wish to sincerely share what I have learned with you. Perhaps I have come at the right time in your life? As they say, "when the sudent is ready, the teacher will appear." Perhaps my story might play a part in your journey? Here is something special for you to think about and work on:

A) What do you want to do to excel?
B) In what ways can you begin to live well with more focused intention?

C) What is your specific goal you are working towards accomplishing at the moment?

D) How can you increase effort to see to the actualization of your dream?

C) What is your specific goal you are working towards accomplishing at the moment?

D) How can you increase effort to see to the actualization of your dreams?

Chapter 3

Challenges

Angela Lee Duckworth, a psychologist at the University of Pennsylvania, teaches that life should be lived as if it were a marathon, not a sprint. The last time I checked, a marathon is a long-distance, rigorous race over an extended period, while a sprint is a short distance, fast run. For you to run a marathon, you have to fully prepare for the experience, build up your physical and mental capacities, and develop the agility to run the race from start to finish. Similarly, life is such a marathon that should be worked out with full purpose, firmness, strength, persistence, and so much more. Because your life marathon is not a short, one-time run. Life should be a daily process that you keep working on, refining day-in and day-out throughout your entire life span. Saint Francis of Assisi suggested, *"Start by doing what's necessary; then do what's possible; and suddenly you are doing the impossible."*

Today, as a man who has graduated with a doctorate degree and has also resuscitated my own business that I abandoned years ago, I love the life that I have. I'm so happy. My life is turning out so good. I crave for more abundance. As I look around at the life I am currently living, I see so many opportunities and strengths in the future. Make no mistake, it didn't just arrive in a sprint, neither have I have already achieved all of my dreams. But I see so many possibilities everywhere in my life's marathon, and I'm happy to make the necessary push for them. I'm walking out the front door each day towards the goals that I've set for myself and am enjoying this journey with my family.

My family means everything to me. They are my reason for doing what I do. I learn so much from them, and I know that as I succeed, it allows me to be able to lay a positive foundation for my kids. My purpose is to provide them a more solid foundation. Let me share a quick secret with you; if you want to excel, live for something special and let that be the motivation that drives you every day to do what you do. Because people who excel know their "why" and it is extremely helpful for you to identify what drives you and to have a deep understanding of *why* you do what you do everyday.

My life has not always been an upward hill experience. I came from a very humble background. I was born and raised in Nigeria before moving to the United States for graduate school. Growing up, our household didn't have much, and our struggle was very real. I knew this because my parents only provided us with the basic necessities of life, and sometimes, these basics were also lacking. We could not afford luxury, or attempt any form of extravagances.

My father was a farmer. He was the main provider in my family. My mother assisted with her little earnings from minimal trading. My father was also skilled in electrical installation, and often he would provide electrical services to private houses and government institutions, but this job was difficult to come by. And so, farming was a major engagement for my family. My father was a brilliant man who worked hard, even in the face of challenges. I learned from him that if I wanted something different, I had to make different choices, and that by doing those things, I could make a difference for my life and family. My dad, no matter what was going on, always told us that things may not be great now, but they're not going to stay this way. His number one philosophy and frequent exhortation to us was to be positive, work hard and everything else will follow.

On the morning of December 31, 1987, my family experienced the worst. I was in a horrible car accident with my father, and three others. The driver, our former neighbor, my step-sister, and my uncle, Nosa. Preceding this tragedy that forever changed my family, on this tragic morning, my father and I had been relaxing under one of the trees at our house. Our house was a beautiful paradise with so many trees that provided us with good shade from the sun's intense heat. As my father and I sat outside enjoying some father and son time, suddenly the driver of the car that almost shattered our lives, a former neighbor of ours, showed up at our residence and stated that he was in the neighborhood visiting and had decided to drop in and say hello to us. After the initial pleasantries, our former neighbor began to chat with my father while I walked away into our house. My action to walk into our house was typical because, in many African cultures, it was considered disrespectful for a child to join in conservation with adults when the child was not invited to join. I later learned from my father that while he and our former neighbor conversed outside, he had asked my father how our family was going to celebrate the coming new year the next day? My father responded to him that we would not be celebrating much because we didn't have food items at home and all that we were stuck and couldn't go to the farm. There was no means for leaving to the farm because my father's car had a mechanical fault and it had not been fixed. Our former neighbor replied with what seemed to me a kind gesture, but the aftermath was catastrophic. He had offered to take my father to the farm in his car. My father accepted the offer and beckoned us with his masculine voice (myself, my stepsister, and uncle) to get ready so we could head to the farm momentarily.

About 40 minutes into our journey to the farm, right as we were approaching a major bridge that has a river on both sides of it, our former neighbor who was driving screamed like a scared child having a really bad nightmare. "Look, an oncoming vehicle is about to collide with us," he shouted. This terrifying scream was surprising because, as far as we could see, no other car was actually coming. I wish we could have seen what he was seeing. That which we did not see remains an untold mystery, but it caused our terrible crash.

Things happened so fast. My father was seated in the front passenger side of the car. Before he could ask our former neighbor who was driving, "are you okay?" or say, "No car is coming!" the driver stepped on his car brakes all at once, full stop. Before we knew what was going on, the car had flipped over and started to turn over multiple times until it eventually stopped. Somehow, the door of the car busted opened and we all fell out like unneeded items thrown off from the trash can. At the time of the accident, my guess would be that the car had been traveling about 65 or 70 miles per hour.Unfortunately, none of us had a seat belt on. I am not sure if wearing seat belts was even a consideration in Nigeria at that time. My father landed with his head directly on the tile-road surface. The center part of his head split with a deep cut and blood started gushing out. Both of his legs were badly broken, as well as his left arm. For me, I landed miles away from the tile-road and ended up in the deep forest. I am not sure how I ended up there in the bush, but I was later rescued and brought to the main scene of the accident where my father and the others were laying helpless. I sustained several internal injuries all over my body.

The doctors later told me that because I was young, that may have been the only reason I made it through the injuries I sustained from the accident. For my father, he wasn't solucky. He suffered from severe complicationsrelated to the accident, and as a result of the crash that day, he died twenty years later.

This accident that almost ended my life occurred around 10:00 am in the morning. We were not transported from the scene of the accident until around 5:30 pm in the evening. Our city emergency services were nowhere to be found, and many motorists that passed by did not stop, while others just peeped at the scene and drove on as if we weren't human beings that needed help. Maybe they were too scared to stop, thinking us to be dead because of the severity of the accident as blood gushed out everywhere. Even if we had been dead, I am not sure what we did to deserve not being helped that day. But I can tell you, we are not the first to experience this kind of man-to-man inhumanity, and we won't probably be the last. It is just human nature, some are good and others maybe not so much.

Remember the story of a man traveling in the Bible who had been robbed and beaten up to the point of near death by thieves? Even a priest of the household of God was among those who saw this wounded fellow and yet deserted him until finally a good fellow came and helped the wounded man. So, human indifference and cruelty have existed for ages, long before you and I were ever born. I have learned that in life, some people will demonstrate compassion and kindness to their fellow human beings, while others have opportunity to improve. So watch out and don't be discouraged, regardless of how you are treated. Be good to others! Even so, wouldn't the world be a better place if everyone could cultivate the attitude of lending a helping hand to each other and rendering to others due benevolence? I think the world could be a magnificent place!

As our accident predicament on the highway persisted with no help in site, it seemed to me like all hope had been lost and we were surely going to perish at the scene. From nowhere, a Good Samaritan finally stopped at the accident scene and transported us to the hospital. The man that day was driving a pick-up truck. We were laying powerless, neary lifeless in the back of that truck. This Good Samaritan who rescued us that day was our major lifesaver. He showed up out of nowhere when we were at the brink of death and is a testament that sometimes in life, when you think all hope is lost, that is when your charming rescue angel will show up to provide you the support and help you need. That support you will receive will, in the end, propel you to the next level despite your odds.

So, I encourage you to do something each day to advance your purpose irrespective of whatever obstacles may stand in your way. Do not allow those obstacles to get the best of you because you never know when your supporting angel will show up and help you cross the finish line. Holocaust survivor, Clara Isaacman said it best: "Everything you do is important because you are exchanging a day of your life for it. Make it count for something purposeful." I wholeheartedly believe this admonition.

Our family's car accident that morning of December 31, 1987, made a bad situation financially worse for my family. My father, who had been the major breadwinner in our family, could no longer provide for us one hundred percent and, we struggled in many areas of our lives. It was truly a difficult time, but we never gave up. Despite my childhood hurdles, in many ways, my early family struggles turned out to become blessings.

You may think I am crazy for stating this, but I tell you, my family's struggles created many opportunities for me to learn about life in ways I might not have. As a result, I am who I am today, because of the lessons from those humble beginnings. Trust me, if you really want to excel irrespective of your background, I suggest you pay crucial attention first to your own life struggles and experiences, and second to the experiences of others. Eduard Christian Lindeman, one of the founding theorists of Adult Education in America stated, *"experience is the richest resource for adults' learning."* Another pioneering scholar of Adult Education in the United States, Malcolm Knowles, who developed the concept of andragogy, put it this way, "*adults learn from experience.*" I could not agree more with both scholars. You want to be learning from the experiences of your life. So be very attentive to your daily experiences and the experiences of others. Reflect on them, because they are valuable lessons that will shape your tomorrow. Remember the popular slogan, "experience is the best teacher." I hope you will let your own experiences become your best teacher. One way to go about this is to work to correct the errors of the past and to pick up new attitudes to shape your future.

Through all of my foundational journey, my father was such a great example to help shape me, because he was always such a very positive force. When he was alive, I remember he would always encourage my siblings and me to focus on the bright side of life, even in the heart of difficulties. This was a novel counsel I constantly received and could hardly comprehend in my youth. Even as a grown man, I still struggle with this admonition today. How do you just focus on the bright side of life when life circumstances can seem so dark at times? But let me be the first to also tell you that I have been saved from many situations by an optimistic disposition. Growing up the way that I did, I learned that no matter what the challenge is that you have in life, those aren't the things that determine what's going to come tomorrow. It is how you perceive and respond to the situation that matters.

Norman Vincent Peale stated, *"How you think about a problem is more important than the problem itself."* Oh, how I love these words.

The life I grew up in has inspired me to want to succeed and to want to do something to make a difference. A difference, not only for my family but also, in the world. As I work with people from diverse backgrounds and help them see the things that they don't see in their life, my hope is that I can live my life as a model for them and through my story, and that they can also live their lives to the fullest.

Most importantly, for my kids and the younger generation that I work with in schools, I want to help them understand how to navigate through their younger years and through college life. I believe that these are the most productive years. If you get it right while you are young, it is hard to miss it in the later years. A lot of mistakes people are struggling with today, stem from their younger years, but that is okay. You have an opportunity to create something special today and for the future.

Lecturer and early childhood development trainer Maria Robinson noted, *"Nobody can go back and make a new beginning, but anyone can start today and make a new ending."* This is another way of saying you cannot dwell on the mistakes of yesterday, but you have the opportunity to make today truly remarkable. So, it is important that young kids and adults learn how to be productive now, to reap the reward of a productive future. Because things in life can become either a springboard, or merely an excuse. For me, I took my humble beginnings and used them to springboard me to so much more. Where I started shaped who I am, but it didn't mean that is how I should end. We grow every day by adding value to ourselves and to the world around us.

A good question to ask is, do you make excuses for your life? If you do, that is okay and it may help you understand why you are where you are, but it cannot lead to excelling. I want you to know excuses are a terrible destroyer of dreams and can rob you of your *responsibility* to excel. To springboard you to success,

here is something special for you to think about and work on:

A) How could you live your life like a marathon?
B) Assess where you started, where are you now, and how do you want your story to be written?
C) What challenges are you facing, and how could you overcome those challenges to become much more?
D) What is your springboard that fuels your daily actions?

Chapter 4

Fighting For Your Life

Life is a gift, and I am thankful for the opportunity to be alive. I am a beneficiary of some of the incredible miracles that occur in human life each day. These daily miracles, no matter how big or small, are often overlooked by many. The truth is that living life with gratitude is such a powerful way of excelling and calling abundance to come into your life. When you appreciate what you have, you get more.

At fifteen, I suddenly became very sick. I was so ill to the point that everyone in my family thought I was going to die. For a whole year I had to stop going to school. My life was on a stand still like a moving train that had suddenly stopped and just quit working. To make matters worse, all the hospitals I was taken to in my locality in Benin City could not figure out what ailed me.

My father knew one Dr. Akele, a medical doctor, who worked at Central hospital in Benin City. She was well respected where we lived. Interestingly, Dr. Akele lived on the same street as our house at that time. She was one of the very few privileged people in our area. We would always whisper about her. We all perceived her as being rich and noble.

Her husband was a lawyer and a gentle dark-skinned man with a natural colorful white hair who loved to go down the street to purchase newspapers on the weekends. They had one daughter everybody wished to be friends with, maybe as a way of benefiting from her parent's wealth, I am not sure. But there is a human tendency to want to associate with those we perceive to be rich and successful. Unfortunately, it was only those with exotic cars that could frolic with Dr. Akele's daughter. She was pretty much a child that was driven from one car to another with a driver standing by. And if you walked with your legs with no car as I had to in my youth, your chances of meeting Dr. Akele's daughter was very slim. Whenever her mother Dr. Akele was driving and coming down the street, people would often point to Dr. Akele's car and say, "look at her the rich doctor coming." Sometimes she quietly drove to her house, ignoring everybody, at other times, she waved her hand to people in the street gazing at her. Maybe, she held the different admiration silent whisper about her. Maybe not. But she did carry herself proudly and well.

Despite her celebrated status, my father was well respected by Dr. Akele. Occasionally, she and her husband would work down the street and stop by at our house to say hello to my father. If I did ever come in contact with her, it was because she would take her time to stop her car and ask me to extend her regards to my father. When they had electrical issues in their house, my father who was skilled in electrical installation and repairs, would help them fix it without collecting money or make them pay for his services, even though they had more than enough to foot the bills. After I became ill, my father went to Dr. Akele because of my condition. She specifically instructed that I should be brought to her hospital for examination. After all the medical examinations and required testing, she could not find what was wrong with me. She stated to my father that she was sad, concerned, and puzzled because, for more than thirty years of her medical practice, she has never seen a case like mine. After a highly gifted professional has spoken, what is left? However, my parents did not give up on me because obviously I was really sick, and they would not allow me to just die without every effort to keep me alive.

I was rapidly losing weight, I couldn't eat nor drink. To even walk was becoming a problem. I was as thin as a broomstick. I was taken to a few other places, and finally, I ended up in my village, a place regarded as my ancestral home town. While at the village, it was all mourning and sadness. For everyone who knew me, the once a charming active boy who was always with his father, now he was just laying down dying and helpless. I held so many whispers and insinuations of what perhaps might have been responsible for my sickness. It didn't matter at this point, all that was needed was a drastic solution. The solution needed to come fast, and it seemed like it was not forthcoming very soon.

In the midst of my predicament and dilemma, my father kinsmen came in and told my parents that the gods weren't happy, and some sacrifices needed to be performed to save my life. You would think quickly my parents, especially my father, whom I was is right-hand son, would jump at the offer to perform sacrifices for me immediately, but not so fast. My father objected and walked off. He stated that he had embraced the Christian faith, and that Christianity forbids performing sacrifices to other gods. I am sure my father's decision that day was a difficult choice. An extremely difficult decision that became remarkable and taught me that in life, I have to stand for something. Otherwise, I might settle for anything. My father's decision that day reminds me of one of Dr. China Achebe's quote that stated, *"One of the truest tests of integrity is its blunt refusal to be compromised."* In this situation my father was not willing to compromise is religious beliefs for something else. In today's world, how often do many people compromise their life to settle for things they don't want. The true reality is that if you want to really excel irrespective of your background, sometimes in life, you have to make some difficult calls and do things many wouldn't do. You have to make some hard choices that challenge your comfort level. At first, you might not even understand why you have to do this, do it anyway because that is the right thing to do that will take you to the next level that you desire. That is how you turn little into more, ordinary to extraordinary, and impossibilities into possibilities. I sincerely wish this to be your experience.

Because my father had fully embraced the Christian faith and was not willing to compromise his religious belief for idol sacrifices, he declared that if God wanted me to survive, so be it, and if not, he was willing to leave my outcome in His hands. This call was questioned by many who thought my father wanted his son to die. I am not sure any man in his right senses, who would ever want his very own blood to perish. I was later brought back from my village to our house in Benin City. I began to receive home therapy and occasionally visited the hospital, while my church members also joined in prayers to pray for my recovery. After about a year of battling this strange illness, slowly, I began to get well again and made the long journey to recovery. I believe God intervened and had mercy on me because my mission on earth was not yet complete. To this day, no one knows why I was sick or what I was sick of. Once I made the journey to recovery, my father later told me that he saw within me the desire to live and how hard I was fighting for my life. I took every medication and followed every process I was asked to undergo, no matter how bitter and difficult it was.

Due to this terrible illness, I had to re-learn how to read, write, and walk all over again at the age of fifteen. I still struggle with how I write and walk to this day. Despite this, I am grateful to be alive to pursue my dreams and aspirations. I came out of this horrible situation a more resilient, confident and determined person. Knowing that no matter what I'd gone through, I was going to be able to make it and live beyond my travails. To be able to look at life situations, no matter how bad, and know that this situation is just temporary is a valuable attitude to have. This attitude is called resilience. The ability for you to be able to draw inner strength to overcome adversity and through the process become valuable to fully shine. One of the amazing lessons I have come to learn was to understand that illness, challenges, setbacks, disappointments, failures, and so on are part of life's unfortunate realities. Not very many people understand this fundamental aspect of life's reality. It will save you a lot of needless worries to understand that life is a mixture of opportunity and difficulties. Sometime you experience the good side of life and at other times, it maybe be challenging. However it is, believe it is well with your soul and take the necessary steps to stay up strong. Problems should be seen as they are, and not elevated with fear. When you experience trials and troubles do not approach challenges already defeated. That is a wonderful phrase right there that you should take special note of, "don't approach challenges already defeated." Can you imagine not putting up effort in a game simply because you already conceived the idea of being defeated? The defeat will be devastating beyond any worse record ever set in human history! Here is what I know that I sincerely wish to impress upon you, challenges are an inevitable part of human experiences. As a result, you must develop and learn specific sets of skills you will utilize to address your own unique challenges when they show up. You cannot quit on yourself, especially not before you even begin to try, because you were born to win. You are meant to triumph, and your success is just around the corner if you are willing to accept the challenge. When afflictions, adversity, and setbacks arrive, compare them cognitively with the different times and seasons of life we all experience. At times it is raining, at other times it is super sunny. One season it is winter which eventually returns to spring. Determine, which season are you experiencing, and then prepare yourself to deal with it accordingly. In addition, I know that challenges do not segregate or discriminate. Everyone has something going on. It would have been nice if life were to always be rosy, but the reality is that it is not. I love quoting Zig Ziglar often, who said, "It's not what happens to you in life that matters. It's how you respond to what happens to you that makes a difference." That is why I believe we have the power to excel within us all. This power is irrespective of where we've come from. Learn to stay in control because you are the master of your own life. Here is something special for you to think about and work on:

A) What is your attitude towards life and how can it be improved?
B) In what ways can you fight for your life?
C) What are the difficult decisions you need to make so you can excel?
D) Challenges are an unavoidable part of the human experience. What skills are you cultivating to help you address your life challenges?

Chapter 5

Despite The Failures: Try Again

After completing my master's degree program in 2012 from Minot State University, I was so optimistic that I was going to commerce my Ph.D. degree studies right away when failure started knocking at my door. I applied to several universities, but I kept getting turned down. After applying to about 10 schools, I gave up and branded myself a failure, relenting to the thought that I wasn't going to be accepted into any school because I was not good enough. I wondered what the point was and why I was wasting my time and paying countless application fees? Mind you, getting a Ph.D. degree had always been my dream, but it didn't seem like it was going to come true. I had given up on this dream so easily. I went about pursuing other endeavors. For the next year and a half, the thought kept coming back to me, reminding me that I had always dreamt of completing my Ph.D. before I turned 40. Why wasn't I going after my dream? This thought was so strong, and it was like something was missing in me that I needed to find. Each time, I read about school or saw anything related to education, like someone graduating from school, the thought of me getting a Ph.D.

would resurface in my mind, thinking, "that could be me." But for the most part, I would just downplay my innermost feelings and continued to ignore what I was feeling inside.

I watch a lot of TED Talks, and I believe I have gained so much inspiration from viewing these videos. They offer more than just browsing the internet without any direction or primary intent. Maybe someday I will deliver a personal TED Talk as part of my to-do bucket list. One beautiful day I was viewing TED Talks videos when I came across a talk by Dr. Ivan Joseph on *"The Skill of Self Confidence."* This talk was so powerful, captivating, and filled with amazing life principles for developing self-confidence. I knew for a fact that if I could implement all that I took away from this talk that day, my life would be so much better. Joseph's talk brimmed with juicy contents on personal and professional growth.

Given that the talk was so captivating to me, I watched it over, and over again. I could not deceive myself that the idea that Dr. Joseph was sharing in his talk wasn't resonating with me. In this presentation, Dr. Joseph, who has a Ph.D. in Sport Psychology, talked about the skill of building self-confidence. Part of this process is the ability to believe that you can accomplish any task no matter the setback, difficulty, and adversity you experience. No doubt, at that point in my life, I was experiencing major setbacks, and my Ph.D. dream seemed to be in jeopardy.

To build self-confidence, Joseph says you have to engage in the process of repetition, repetition, and repetition. In other words, you have to repeat, repeat, and repeat a particular exercise over again and again to gain mastery and confidence irrespective of the odds. He went further to note, there are many people who quit. Other people brand themselves as a failure when they experience first defeat and adversity. In particular, this was not my first defeat or first time experiencing adversity. And it probably wouldn't be my last. But I likened the talk to my current experience of trying to get into a Ph.D. program. I was encountering setbacks.

Hearing that you have to repeat a particular process over and over again despite feeling defeated helped me to develop a line of action to bounce back. Although I was curious how many times you needed to repeat a process before actually quitting. I don't have a good answer to that, so I will leave it to expert researchers. What was relevant to my progress was that I learned not to quit so easily. Michael Jordan, America's greatest basketball player noted, *"I have missed more than 9000 shots in my career. I've lost almost 300 games. 26 times, I've been trusted to take the game winning shot and missed. I've failed over and over and over again in my life. And that is why I succeed."* This quote gives us the insight into why we can never quit. So, to develop self-confidence, you have to practice,

practice, and practice and not accept failure as a result. As I listened to all Dr. Joseph said, it seemed for a second, that he was speaking to me. Have you ever had one of those weird moments of trepidation when someone is delivering a speech, and it seems like your story had been told to the speaker? And now you are just being bombarded? That was how I felt that day, as I saw myself in the speech. The only difference was that I was interpreting and processing the message for my own good. Dr. Joseph's talk was all I needed to hear at that time in my life to revive my Ph.D. ambition, and truly the talk did just that. After listening to this presentation over and over again, I decided I was going to give my Ph.D. dream another shot. I then decided to apply one more time, in complete defiance against my own negative self-talk and thoughts. But if I was going to build my confidence, I would have to humble myself and apply action to my dream. Because, as the great Normal Vincent Peale noted, *"Action is a great restorer and builder of confidence."* I wasn't going to let the fear of rejection create inaction for me or to erode my confidence. I was ready to act. Again.

I started all over again. I started searching and applying to graduate schools. I redrafted my statement of purpose, gave it to a friend of mine to look at it. He felt it was the coolest statement of purpose he had ever read after a few twists. The first school I applied to after my eleventh application responded in the affirmative, and I got accepted! Imagine how I felt the day I opened my mail and discovered that I have been admitted to study for a Ph.D. at North Dakota State University. I immediately suspended other applications and started preparing to attend graduate school again. After the initial euphoria and excitement of being accepted for a Ph.D. program, the reality set in again. That negative voice and sucker of dreams that you should never allow to dwell in you for too long before you immediately banish it away, once you recognize it returning. I started to ask myself limiting questions. How on earth am I going to do this? Why do I need to undergo this Ph.D. journey, and so on and so forth? I remembered that first night of class when I started my Ph.D. program and how I did not understand any of the terms that were used in class. The professor in class, Dr. Brent Hill, who later became my good friend, was using complex terms such as paradigms, epistemology, and conceptual framework. He quoted lots of academic literature in class, asking questions such as, have any of you read this book, have you read that? He closed the class that day by giving us an extensive list of readings that we were presumably supposed to read within a very short period of time. After receiving all of the information and at the conclusion of my first doctoral class, my mind set back, I panicked, and obviously entered into the zone of what I call "*choice proximity of self-doubt.*" A period when you voluntarily decide to doubt your abilities.

At this time, I was questioning myself repeatedly, "How can I do this? How will I have the ability to be able to undergo this program?" I made all kinds of excuses, "I'm not well read. Why do I want to do this? In the midst of all this fight with myself, I learned the next day that I was not going to be receiving any form of financial assistance, or scholarships, not even a graduate assistantship that was supposed to alleviate my financial burden a bit. A couple of days later, I went into my assigned doctoral advisor's office at that time. Dr. Elizabeth Roumell who now teaches at Texas A & M University in College Station. I went in with the mind of telling her that I was going to quit my Ph.D. program because I wasn't getting any financial assistance. Was that really the main problem? I don't think that it was. I doubted my potential, and wondered whether I was sure I would actually succeed? Anyways, I proceeded with all my excuses and complained about not been giving financial assistance. I asked her how I am supposed to do this program without any funding. I have a young family that I also need to provide for. To my amazement, she carefully listened to me, and after my narratives, she told me if I really want to do this I have to make some sacrifices and the effort would worth my time, but it was absolutely my decision and my call. She went ahead and shared with me her own personal doctoral education journey and related how in her first year of graduate school she went as far as working low paying jobs to fund her education and sometimes she worked very early in the morning before going to class. Added to this, she had three kids she was caring for by herself. After hearing the story of my advisor that I admire so much, I came out from the meeting with the resolve that day that if my advisor can do it, then I should try to do it. I was going to do this, come what may. You would think that it was this easy, just by saying I was going to do this. Honestly, there were times up to the last day I defended my dissertation that I still considered seriously quitting. Throughout my Ph.D. journey, I came to learn that talk is cheap. It is action that is hard, but valuable. If you combine both, you have something very special to excel.

Besides my first doctoral advisor's story that inspired me, I learned from my first cohort gathering that a lot of well qualified potential applicants applied to this program, but only fourteen of us were accepted into the program. I thought for a second, "So, apparently, I was good enough." I may not be seeing myself the way others were perceiving me. This was reinforced months later, as a first-year doctoral student, I had applied to present a research paper at a conference, and my paper was accepted. I later learned that over a hundred papers were submitted for the conference, mine was one of the few that was accepted. This message still sticks with me today. It carried me through my entire Ph.D. program. Every time I doubted myself, I came back to: "I was one of the fourteen admitted into a PhD., program, apparently, I am good enough." We often do not see ourselves the same way others perceive us to be.

While I was studying for my Ph.D., I was working two additional jobs in order to meet the obligations of providing for my family. Often, this felt like it was too much to manage. I would frequently drift into the oblivion of self-doubt and question myself: "Why am I doing this?" "Am I going to be able to do this?" I remember many nights coming home, at 2:00 a.m., after both working and having gone to school, and my wife would ask me to go to the store to pick up items we did not have at home. In the dead cold heart of the North Dakota snow, I would still head to the store to get what we needed. Sometimes it just felt like it was too much for me. I can't count how many times I wanted to stop. I had to learn how to have positive conversations with myself. I needed to remind myself what it was that I was pushing for. I worked on myself often. In fact, to this day, I keep working on myself. Each time I would doubt myself, I remembered my father studied every night. I remembered his encouragement to me. I remembered many of his wise counsels. Then I would remember that I was one of only fourteen students out of many that had been accepted. You see, you are good enough regardless of the negative thoughts you think about yourself or where you've come from.

Four years later, I successfully ended my Ph.D. engagement being second to finish out of the cohort of fourteen original people that started the program. My Ph.D. journey was a struggle, but I did it and gained a lot from the life-changing experience, so much so, that if I were to ever get a chance to do it again, sure, I would jump at the opportunity. Through this experience, I learned that I have the power to do the things that I doubted, and I want you to know that you can do it too. I have always believed and correctly stated that you don't know how far you can go in life if you don't try. I have proven myself to be right with my own experience, and I hope I continue to prove myself right. So, if you have any goal you wish to accomplish try your best, if your approach doesn't work the first time, try again, and again, and again until you finally succeed. We all have within us the power to excel despite where we come from or our experience. Norman Vincent Peale stated, *"Believe in yourself. Have faith in your abilities. Without a humble, but reasonable, confidence in your own powers, you cannot be successful or happy."* I believe this to be true. Frankly, if you don't believe in yourself who else will? There is already multitudes of people out there who will judge you, and who will tell you can't do it. Why play into their hands? Why allow someone else to decide your power and how far you can go in life? They don't know you, nor the limit of your potential? God created you to succeed. America's Motivational sensational speaker, Les Brown said, *"someone's opinion of you, does not have to become your reality."* So, live your dreams.

I really had to deal with my own negative thoughts and push myself a little bit more regardless of what others thought. People often live out the negative voices of others, including their own, instead of following their personal desired path. Personally, I had a tendency to be a person who thought negatively when things happened, and this attitude seemed to get in the way of my ultimate goal at the time. I had to work on this, and I feel so much better when I give it a try and don't doubt myself. There is power in our thoughts. Here is something special for you to think about and work on:

A) What music is playing in your head? Do you tell yourself "I am good enough?"
B) What is your attitude towards failure? How can you improve it and, if necessary, change it?
C) What do you watch? Are they inspiring and empowering your course? Try some TED TALKS!
D) What are some ways you can push yourself a little bit more to excel?

Chapter 6

Perception & Productivity

My father was a farmer, but unfortunately, I never liked going to the farm. I remember when I was a teenager, my parents would take my siblings and me to the farm on some weekends and more frequently once school was on holiday. Unluckily for me in particular, regardless that I never really loved going to the farm, my father would always prefer me to go with him. If a choice was to be ever made about who should go to the farm among my siblings, the dice would fall on me. So I was stuck with my father in a party I could never leave. One major reason I did not like farming at the time was because I had naively conceived farming only from a shallow perception of it being difficult. I didn't really see the point. On the other hand, I forgot all the benefits that came with farming, including the reality that we didn't have to buy much because we grew our own food. I still don't forget how I screamed in Walmart one day when I picked a bag of oranges and noticed the price tag. For my entire life up to about 28 years, I had never bought fruit because we grew a variety of fruit on our own. I was stunned to learn how expensive fruit are for purchase. Across America today, more than six million children need food or don't know where the next meal will come from, and there I was downplaying the reward of farming that was the livelihood for my family. It isn't so much that farming is really that difficult, it's just like any other profession, you have to learn the skills in order to be able to do it well.

One day, my father wanted us to go to the farm, and I did not want to go. I am not sure whether, in all my life, if I knew how to say no to my father without getting into trouble, but on this occasion it was just like I did not care. The look on my face said it all, as I displayed a really grumpy face. Although this was very typical of me in those days when it was time to go farming, on this particular occasion my father wasn't having it, and wasn't going to let the moment slide by without him showing his tough love and wise words of counsel. He had noticed for a long while, whenever it was time to head to the farm, that my negative attitude towards farming would be in full display. On that day, he made sure he used his response to teach me the lesson that would forever impact me for the rest of my life. This life-changing lesson was in the form of lecture-scolding. You know many people don't care much for lectures, even though it is a proven instructional method. I, in particular, when the lecture was too long, would just fall asleep. But when my father had something to say whether long or short, who was I to not listen? As I displayed my grumpy outlook when it was time to head to the farm, the boss of the house, my father said to me with a sharp tone:

*"You don't have to go to the farm if you don't want to, for your **perception will determine your productivity**. If you ever think your adventure from a negative perspective, it will blindfold you to its benefits, reduce your energy and the commitment you put into it and in such circumstances the odds of you succeeding is little if not impossible. On the other hand, if you are positive and optimistic about what you do, it will increase your energy, create in you great passion, and in such a situation, success is your credentials. So, just*

> *stay home if you don't want to go, because I don't want your attitude to become a liability for me today while we are out there."*

I am not trying to trick you into the often-common motivational punch line you hear from some speakers that if you just think positive, that is everything you need in life. That is not true, although I think you would benefit more from positive thinking than negative thinking. It does indeed help in many life situations to stay positive. If you assume the best you get the best. If you imagine the worst the worst happens. There is a fundamental difference between that fellow who sees life from a bright side, despite its ups and downs, and one who possesses all the negativity in the world at the slightest difficulty. After my father's scolding and tough love, all I literally hear, to this day, is the sound bite in my ears, "*You don't have to if you don't want to, but your **perception will determine your productivity**.*" Wow, what a message, my perception will determine my productivity. No wonder, Henry Ford once stated: "*Whether you think you can, or think you can't, you are right.*" Absolutely, how you think, and perceive life events will determine a lot about your projected outcome. So, because of my negative attitude towards farming, my father literally used the moment to help me understand that the outlook I carry about my life engagements will drive my productivity and outcomes.

That is the coolest way to describe optimism. Come to think about it, how possible could it be to get to the top if you don't think you can make it? Your guess is as good as mine! Throughout my life, I have witnessed what an optimistic attitude can do, and how it can literally change everything you do and your perspective on life, irregardless of your present situation. John Maxwell, the leadership expert, stated, *"attitude is the difference maker in your life."* I do believe this quote to be true. The very foundation that built this country, America, and drove her to prominence in the nineteenth century was built on the positive premise of optimism. With a wave of immigrants: Men and women mostly fleeing persecution and fueled by the determination and hope that, despite trials and adversity, a better life is attainable in the new world. That is how immigrants moved to America to build a new home, as a result of their hope and positive expectations. This is how the United States came to be referenced as a nation of optimists.

I recall, when I was growing up and things were very challenging for my family, how my father would often say to us, "Guys, I know that the finances of the family aren't too great right now, notwithstanding, each and every one of you are going to be great, I see a brighter future for all of you my children. You are going to have everything you need in life to be successful, just hold your heads right, be optimistic, and work hard for your future." At first, I never understood what my father meant, because I could not see it. Yes, we were poor, and things needed to change. I was like, "Come on daddy, what are you talking about?" But let me also be the first to confess to you that despite the situation of things, my father was a very positive man who would only focus on the bright side of things, even in difficult circumstances. Whenever there was hard work to do in the house, he would be the first to show up and motivate others to come help. So hearing those kinds of optimistic statements from him so often, that things would get better, contagiously conditioned my mind to be confident about my future. It also helped me to stay positive in life, despite my challenging background. Somehow, I just had the belief that things were going to turn out right for me, and that feeling has guided every action of mine to this very day. Although my vulnerability and the weaker side of my humanity tries to get the best of me sometimes, I am fighting it each day because I know I am unrelenting, and I know you can be too. Later, I came to understand how my father could speak so optimistically towards our future, and it has played out accordingly.

When you are optimistic, you get more out of your life than when you dabble in pessimism. An optimist sees light at the end of the tunnel, while a pessimist sees a dead-end. Of course, there are actual dead-ends in life, but I encourage you to consider re-framing them. When you choose the latter, you tend to see only the worst in people and life's situations. This is the fastest road to depression and loneliness. I can't imagine you would want to hire a negative person who only sees the downfall of your business in the future. Conversely, you would give uttermost consideration to that applicant who has a positive world view and bright vision for your company.

If this is true, I think optimism is a great attitude to carry in your own life. Everyone could use a little bit of optimism in life. Optimism is a positive way of thinking about the causes of events in your life and maintaining a hopeful attitude for a best possible outcome, rather than excessive worrying. It is an approach to life that envisions things will get better rather than fretting that, "I am doomed forever." Winston Churchill, the famous British Prime Minister during World War II, once stated, *"A pessimist sees the difficulty in every opportunity; an optimist sees the opportunity in every difficulty."* This is very correct. People with the ability for optimistism tend to fight off life challenges, and they exercise toughmindedness. It is a great recipe to increase mental health and reduce depression. The mental image you carry does play a significant role in how you feel and act. When the negative thoughts come in, which is the direct opposite of optimism, you must actively think and ask yourself, "Why am I thinking this negatively?" Ask yourself, "What is the best possible outcome that can come out of this?" When you engage in this

Socratic practice, you are on the path to developing self-realization and self-awareness.

Furthermore, being optimistic does not mean that you deny the realities of your life, optimism simply emphasizes hoping for and working toward the best possible outcome. This approach will help you handle life events better; rather than letting life events handle you. If you constantly come from a negative attitude, you will have a negative result. We all need to learn how to beat down those negative internal conversations because they beat you down. Sometimes this will be your greatest challenge. Sometimes the negative side seems so much easier, but as we learn to beat the habitual negative thoughts down through an optimistic approach, we learn how to overcome adversity from a positive light and build our confidence through action.

Here is something special for you to think about and work on:

A) How do you approach each day?
B) What attitude do you need to develop to help you stay productive?
C) Observe how you mostly think to determine whether it is an optimistic or pessimistic style of thinking? Make the necessary changes as it suits your situation.
D) Interpret two challenging events in your life from the best possible outcome, and continue to do this until you are comfortable treating

all events from the best possible outcome.

Chapter 7

How Success Works

Each time I have the privilege to speak at a conference, I try to begin and make the self-disclosure that I was originally born and raised in Nigeria before moving to the United States. I do this because I have discovered that I repeatedly get asked three questions, one of which is, "How I do like the United States given I have a different cultural background?" After a moment of what seems like a mild smile on my face, I will respond to this question with great passion and enthusiasm that, despite all that is going on with issues of racism and serotypes, I do indeed love the United States, It is the best place to be, and I have found a home here. My love for the United States is not attributed to silver, nor gold, but if there was, I might as well search for it, work hard and smart to benefit from the precious silver and gold that is as important like oxygen. My affection for this country is rooted in the philosophical foundations that built this nation. This foundation is entrenched in the idea that, no matter where you are from or what your background looks like, you have a shot at the American dream if you work tirelessly with purpose, hope, and determination. American historian who coined the phrase *American Dream*, James Truslow Adams, elaborately described this American dream this way:

"The American Dream is that dream of a land in which life should be better and richer and fuller for everyone, with opportunity for each according to ability or achievement. It is not... a dream of motor cars and high wages merely, but a dream of social order in which each man and each woman shall be able to attain to the fullest stature of which they are innately capable, and be recognized by others for what they are, regardless of the fortuitous circumstances of birth or position."

James Truslow Adam's quote is a confirmation of the repeated theme I have stated throughout this book, that everyone has the power to excel irrespective of their background. This is true because how you were born does not necessarily determine what you become in life. Most of the world's greatest from Abraham Lincoln to Nelson Mandela, Mohammad Ali, Frederick Douglass, Steve Job, Samuel Walton, Mother Teresa, Rosa Parks, Oprah Winfrey, and many others had a humble beginnings. Everyone can learn from their humble beginnings and legacies.

About a decade ago, when I first arrived in the United States, a friend of mine called me a few days later to welcome me to America. He asked me how my long flight was. I told him it was great and that New York City is beautiful and simply amazing. After exchanging our initial salutations, we both began to talk over the phone about life in America. My friend asked me if I saw the popular bank-tree in New York. I responded no, after a short pause, I asked him what kind of tree that is? He said to me it is a type of tree that bears actual money like fruits and people just stop there to grab whatever amount of money they needed from the tree. At the time, I almost fell for his prank because he was dead serious and said to me I've missed something huge and he is very disappointed. I was supposed to stop at the popular tree-bank spot and gather all the actual money I needed. I kept quiet for a minute, thinking how am I supposed to know?

After a short silence, I gathered my thoughts and asked my friend why he hasn't gone to this popular tree-bank to get all that he needed if such a supernatural tree that bears real money existed? I knew for a fact that he would be the first person to be there if such a tree ever existed. At this point, he started laughing. At the same time, he had nothing to say back to me because he knew, I caught him in his sarcastic prank. I later learned from my friend that was his way of indirectly telling me about the struggle that is real right here in America, and that you don't get money sitting down somewhere in the streets, you have to work hard for every dollar you get. Although this was meant to be a joke, there is truthfulness in my friend's indirect sarcasm that you don't get money sitting down somewhere in the streets. Of course, I know that. I first heard through the song of Majek Fashek, the Nigerian reggae singer of the 1980s, that there are beggars in the streets of New York. Truly, when I first arrived in New York and was about to board a bus ride, a fellow approached me and beckoned on me to give him a dollar. This was stunning to me, because all of the images we see outside the United States of it being a perfect society were gold just litters the streets. How could we possibly still find people who are begging and homeless? Let's get real, right!?!

One of the simple but remarkable lessons I have learned from coming to the United States is the idea that, whether you're in the United States, Nigeria, England,

France, Mexico, or anywhere really, there is no easy path to success. It is just that some countries are better organized than others. These countries set you up for success if you are ready to go for it. However, I have come to understand that wherever you are, you need to work hard, be optimistic, have the right philosophy and system in place to help you achieve, and live your dreams. The principle of working hard dates back to Adam and Eve in the scriptures. When you are outside the United States, it's so easy to think that when you come to the U.S., things are going to be easier all at once. That isn't necessarily the truth. Wherever you are from and whatever your background is, you have your own destiny to design. Success doesn't recognize where you are from, but does indeed recognize your vision and tireless efforts and tenacity to excel. So you are the one who has to decide what you want and make it happen. Dr. Joseph, whose Ted Talk I cited earlier stated that you are the "*captain of your own ship.*" First, you have to understand who you are, and then you have to understand what you're diving into next. Often, we don't know how deep the sea is that we're diving into. We may need to be better equipped before we dive in, so that we have the ability, no matter how deep the water is, to swim and find our way to success. This analogy also works in approaching your life. You must understand how life is and prepare all your necessary tools to navigate life's complexity.

No one, except infants, comes from a clean slate. The things that have happened in our past are there. The challenges that we've faced, and will face, are all part of life. Even as we go through rough times, we have to understand that these hard times won't last. It is the challenges that actually help us grow and really bring out who we are. Shortly before he died, the American civil right icon Dr. Martin Luther King, Jr. stated: *"The ultimate measure of a man [woman] is not where he [she] stands in moments of comfort and convenience, but where he [she] stands at times of discomfort and challenges."* How insightful is this quote? Anyone can handle moments of comfort and joy, but that is not the true test of your character. It is during trials and turmoil that a person's courage is put to the test. That is when you grow and get to really know who you are.

Remember the biblical story of the stinking rich man name Job? When he became very sick and lost all his possessions and maids? He was instructed by his spouse to curse God so he could reclaim his wealth back. He refused and rebuked her, stating, "can one eat sweet and not taste bitter?" Of course not; life is full of bittersweet moments, but for you to succeed you must be ready to show tough character and stay strong during challenging times. Be aware that most of the time, people need to experience tough times in order for them to grow and learn. Why is that? I don't know, but that is how life works. Therefore, do not wish that your challenges were fewer, rather wish for the wisdom and skills to navigate your challenges. Also, it is true that tough times really offer you a chance to know who you are and to cultivate your resilient spirit. These things are not easy. I guarantee you, but the reality is that you need to approach the challenges that life throws your way constructively in order for you to succeed.

So, there are no more excuses, no more taking the easy way out by saying, "Well, I don't have this or that to reach what I want." Excuses are easy. Challenge yourself to see just how much your life can change for the better. We all need to be actively searching for our next opportunity to excel. Challenging yourself to go beyond what you are used to can provide that opportunity. Success is there if you're not making excuses for why you can't succeed. We must push forward, but not by seeking the easy road. In fact, be careful and watchout suspiciously for anything that comes too easy. Success is not a one time affair, but a life time opportunity.

As I mentioned earlier in this book, life is like a marathon. It is important to understand that success is not just a phenomenon you suddenly stumble upon. Rather, success is a process, a daily exercise of becoming, and over time it will be reflected in your journey and accolades. America's foremost business philosopher, Jim Rohn, simplified it best, *"Success is nothing more than a few simple disciplines, practiced every day."* This is so true because as you consistently work on your chosen discipline each day, you become, you better your best, and it just keeps getting better by the day. It doesn't matter who you are and where you are from; as you approach success as daily matters, the law of averages will cause a ratio to appear, and that ratio will be a story of excellence.

When I first started delivering public presentations, you should have seen me. For lack of a better word to describe my performance, I will just simply state, I was horrible. When I mean bad, I was just terribly bad. But I have a tendency not to stop once I have set a goal to accomplish. So, I just kept working on my speaking every day because I know I have this gift to impact others with words, it will serve me and the world better if I utilize this strength. I am absolutely convinced I can become better. I am still working on me every day. I still have not reched the place where I want to be, but every day I am learning the things that will help me get better, and I work on it one day at a time.

Despite my inadequacies, my greatest joy is that after I finish a presentation, I still get someone who will come to me and "say thank you for speaking, I enjoyed your speech, and I learned something." I am the one who knows I need to get better, because I don't just want to be good, I want to excel in the art of public speaking. Recently, I spoke to a group of high school students. During the presentation, I made mention of the need for students to figure out why they are going to college. It is a question to help students find their purpose. After the presentation, a student walked up to me with emotion and stated I have been struggling with this, but you have helped me re-focus myself today. As weird as my voice might sound, I shared a message, and my message was well received. This is the kind of motivation and joy that keeps me going and wanting to do more.

If you are not comfortable with where your life currently is, keep working on it to try to make things better, because your success is just around the corner. Over time with consistency, the natural consequence of doing something persistently will manifest. Alan Cohen

Stated, *"Do not wait until the conditions are perfect to begin. Beginning makes the conditions perfect."* I am not sure if there is a perfect condition for you on this earth, all I know and can guarantee you is that your journey will only get better if you work hard and long enough to silence your innermost fears. The funny comedian and filmmaker, Louis C.K. stated, *"I've learned from experience that if you work harder at it, and apply more energy and time to it, and more consistency, you get a better result. It comes from the work."* This is absolutely true, Louis. All that is being emphasized is that you must be willing to put forth the effort, sufficient enough to stop you from making excuses. I know for a fact that an excuse is a terrible killer of dreams.

Here is something special for you to think about and work on:

A) What does it mean to you to work tirelessly to reach your goal?
B) What is your life's personal philosophy and mission? Write it out so you can see.
C) What systems do you have in place to help you succeed?
D) What are you willing to do to excel beyond your background, even in the midst of challenges?

Chapter 8

Voice of Hope

I would like to become a voice of encouragement and offer you a couple of additional thoughts. If you have been reading closely, you will realize that the experiences and insights I have shared with you thus far in this book offer insight and inspiration to help you navigate your own life experiences. I have given you clues on how to address the many odds of life, so you can excel. As I gradually round up with some concluding insights, I believe now is a good time for you to make the necessary leap, go to work, to make your dreams a reality by applying the principles you have learned from reading this book. One of the things I will encourage is not to make excuses. You should not make excuses for your life, as you do have all that it takes to reach your potential. We all are blessed with the same 24 hours a day, the difference is that some utilize their time well, while others have the opportunity to become more effective with their time. So, you just need to challenge yourself a little bit more, and you will be amazed at the results of what you can do. Undeniably, if you really want to succeed beyond all expectations, you must develop the grit to take life head on and avoid the game of making excuses that most people play. It is very important that you avoid excuses because it can create a wall of denial for you and block your pathway forward. People who succeed FOUND A WAY, and those who do not succeed MAKE EXCUSES. Barack Obama, 44th President of the United States once stated, *"The best way to not feel hopeless is to get up and do something. Don't wait for good things to happen to you. If you go out and make some good things happen, you will fill the world with hope, you will fill yourself with hope."*

Absolutely, we all need hope to excel. I don't care if you like former president Barack Obama, or not, or whether you thought he was a great president or good one. But I can assure you that this is an amazing thought from former Mr. President. If you implement this single quote as it is written, it is not going to be very long and you will find yourself excelling. As John Maxwell noted, *"achievement comes from good habit,"* and I think the habit of finding a way to excel and not making excuses is a good habit. A lot of the time, it's so easy to just say, "I am not from a rich home," "I do not have this, or I do not have that." This accounts for the reason why my life is in a downward spiral. While there may be a thousand reasons to account for failure, there is no reason good enough for you not to have tried to achieve your purpose. The truth is that if you want to separate yourself from the crowd that is already down at the bottom, and sought that others join them below; I urge you, do not make excuses. Rather actively look for opportunities to excel and to improve yourself each day. John Maxwell, in "Thinking For A Change," stated, *"success comes to those who will habitually do the things unsuccessful people won't do."* Indeed, to excel is to succeed; and success in retrospect is defined by the impactful things you do daily that are getting you closer to your dreams. I just believe your dream is too powerful never to be realized. A good question to begin with is: What am I doing today that will shape my tomorrow for the better?

Another idea I would also like to reiterate to you as you develop the habits to excel, is to be very optimistic about your life. I can never emphasize enough the value of having a positive outlook on life. Because a negative outlook on life is a fast route to hopelessness and a dead-end. If you interact with some people who are highly depressed or experiencing suicidal tendencies, you may be shock to discover that those situations of miseries did not just suddenly show-up. My personal opinion is that it happened from a series of accumulated negative emotions. I am not saying if you have a medical condition, you can just positively think your way back to health. You have to follow a stipulated path to recovery. In addition, your being positive does significantly help in this long journey to recovery. Against the commonly held assumption by some that if you just think positive, that is all you need to succeed. I don't quite subscribe to that idea and disagree with this very notion. But I will also be the first to tell you that there is power in your own thoughts and how you perceive the things in your life is extremely significant to your success. I know this well from my personal life experiences. If I did not maintain a positive outlook on life, I would not be sitting here at my table writing this book you are reading, given all I have encountered in my life. Anybody can write a book, but the how you think about the actual art of writing makes all the difference. So, I think it is of tremendous help to maintain a positive outlook about your life regardless of what your current experiences may be. No one is telling you that it is going to be easy with all the challenges and negativity in this world, or that is is challenging us to not to fall back into being pessimistic. However, there is something very special and transformational with how you see life when you choose to think about your life from a positive viewpoint.

Observe your thoughts closely and do not take how you feel for granted. Optimism produces joy, confidence, assurance, peace of mind, commitment, and hope to live life to its fullest. While the reverse of these qualities may as well be the case in the absence of optimism. Imagine two people born into this world with similar experiences and background. One went about to do extraordinary things worth commending and the other you wonder what happened. A good place to unpack their lives is to check how optimistic they each were about their life. What I would say to anybody out there who really wants to thrive in life, is to remain very optimistic, because your thoughts will have a significant effect in determining your energy and how you approach the beautiful life you have been given.

As you have read in my personal account, I was having these challenges within myself, but having the ability to hear those optimistic words from my father over and over again; *"My perception determines my productivity,"* helped me to be able to understand myself and to be able to teach myself to be optimistic. It was optimism that brought me to America, despite not knowing how things were going to turn out. It was optimism that helped me to try again when I lost sight of my Ph.D. goal and was experiencing rejections. It was optimism that helped me to bounce back to life when I became terribly ill, and everybody in my family thought I was going to die at the age of fifteen. It was optimism that helped my family to progress when we did not have enough and did not know where our next meal would come from. Even in those difficult times, my mother will still share the little we had with somebody else in more need. How crazy the good things people just do. From a humble beginning, I was ready to explore my destiny and turn things around in good faith. Similarly, you can begin to identify what optimism has done for you, and you will experience the power in optimistic living.

The normal flow of things is clear, if you don't think that you can get to the top, then you're probably not going to get to the top. You have heard, as a man thinketh so he is. On the brighter side, if you think you'll get to the top, there is no stopping you, whatever happens, keep aiming for the top, then reaching that top becomes something achievable.

To begin the process of moving forward today, I advise you to implement the following:

(a) Learn to be optimistic regardless of your life circumstance or experience;

(b) Understand challenges are a part of everyone's life reality, and try to devise a skill to address your current challenges;

(c) When you experience a setback at something, try again;

(d) Live your life with purpose and good intentions; and lastly

(e) Always have a goal that you are working towards. Once you achieve this goal, start another one, and another one, and another one, and before you know it, you are on a much higher ground than where you originally began.

This process is so rewarding and remarkable. I hope you experience this process.

In closing, I would like to ask you to be determined, and not to give up on yourself, come what may. A lot of the time when people are experiencing challenges, the easy way they deal with the situation is to give up. This is why we have so many unaccomplished dreams and unachieved intentions. Nobody's life is 100% challenge free. The world wasn't created without trials and adversities. Jesus Christ, the uniquely selected son of God experienced adversity. At a point, he even had to cry out to His father, our father God, and he asked why has "thou forsaken me?" It wasn't that master J. was really forsaken, it was just the pain of challenges he experienced that made it seem so. This pain is very real in all of us. I know something about that, and I know that you know something about pain as well. But there is a special power and unique feeling when we are able to stand tall and overcome those pains. Overcoming adversity is the number one way you can excel. So, when you are experiencing those difficult moments, I encourage you to hold strong! Figure out within yourself the best things that will help you to not just survive, but to thrive in situations. The queen of poetry, the late Maya Angelou, said it best, *"My mission in life is not merely to survive, but to thrive, and to do so with some passion, some compassion, some humor, and some style."* This quote is absolutely gorgeous that we need to think beyond merely surviving.

Unfortunately, surviving is the life that most people live, just scraping to get by and trying to make it through the day. In fact, we live and work in a culture of "just dealing" and struggling our way through the day. Does it have to be this way? We can raise our own bar higher and make a conscious effort to live a life toward thriving. This can only be achieved when we do not take our eyes off our goals. Theodore Roosevelt admonishes, *"do what you can, with what you have, where you are."* So, have a goal of what you want to do and be focused on changing your life with it. The idea is for you to continuously move to the next level, which is your key to success and excelling.

I remember after completing my Ph.D., degree, a lot of people around me were asking the same questions. In fact, my wife was the first person to ask me: "What is next? What do you want to do now?" I personally asked myself the same questions. "Okay, now that I have completed this journey, what is my next goal?" "What do I need to accomplish next?" That is when I thought, I need to write this book, I have had a desire for too long to share my story with the world. I just believe for you to excel irrespective of your background, you should constantly be setting goals of what you desire to do next. It is like adding oil to your lamp for you to recharge and see what is ahead of you. Because for you to move to the next level, you can't just rely on your past success. It is like yesterday. Your yesterday is past, and tomorrow is very promising. As a result, you must always be looking ahead and moving forward. You need to continue to break new walls. Setting goal after goal and accomplishing them will help you in this direction.

At times, this might not be the easiest thing to do, but you need to remain determined, resilient, and optimistic. No matter what life throws at you, be committed to seeing things through. Especially those things that will move you to the next level. Nigerian literature icon, Wole Soyinka once said, *"The hand that dips into the bottom of the pot will eat the biggest snail."* What a wise idiomatic expression. The truth is that you don't know when you will catch your big snail, or when your next big moment is to come. Keep working like it will be this very day. But as the idiom stipulates, first you will have to gather the courage and conviction to dip your hand into the bottom of the pot, and then you come out with a big snail. This is what I believe life expects from us. In fact, it is stated in the Holy books that you must ask, and then you receive. It is just the natural law of nature and how things work. During this process of asking, like dipping your hand into the bottom of the pot, that is when you get your breakthrough moments. The problem is that sometimes we are afraid to dip into the bottom of the pot for fear of failure. So, I challenge you, not to be afraid, no matter what life throws at you, dip your hand into the pot of life, be determined, and committed to your success. Through determination and commitment, you can surely make it through the stormy days of life. Because you know what, you are unstoppable, and you do have the power to excel irrespective of your background. Thank you for taking this journey with me.

Here is something special for you to think about and work on:

A) What are your major take aways from this book that will help you to navigate your journey?
B) What necessary leap are you going to make after reading this book?
C) How do you plan to excel?
D) How will you handle adversity when you experience difficulty?

Chapter 9: Special Reflection

"Life is an opportunity, benefit from it. Life is beauty, admire it. Life is a dream, realize it. Life is a challenge, meet it. Life is a duty, complete it. Life is a game, play it. Life is a promise, fulfill it. Life is sorrow, overcome it. Life is a song, sing it. Life is a struggle, accept it. Life is a tragedy, confront it. Life is an adventure, dare it. Life is luck, make it. Life is too precious, do not destroy it. Life is life, fight for it."

~ *Mother Teresa*